Out of the

A New Life in the Devc

by Sonya O'Donognue

Copyright © Sonya O'Donoghue

ORCHARD PUBLICATIONS
2 Orchard Close, Chudleigh, Newton Abbot, Devon TQ13 0LR
Telephone: (01626) 852714

All rights reserved. No part of this publication may
be reproduced, stored in a retrieval system, or transmitted in any form or by
any means, without the prior permission of the copyright holder.

ISBN 1 898964 26 2

Designed, Typeset and Printed for Orchard Publications by
Swift Print
2 High Street
Dawlish
Devon EX7 9HP

Chapter

1

Bramble Cottage

"ATTENTION, ATTENTION, THEFT IN PROGRESS," - over and over again. For the umpteenth time our van carrying all our daily stock requirements was being broken into.

"Dave I've had enough of this, we've got to get away," I cried in desperation.

For months we had become increasingly disillusioned with London life, with the difficulties of trying to run a small business and the coming to terms with watching our way of life and the every day standards of behaviour, which we were brought up to believe in, being swept away and replaced by greed, by aggression and destruction. We'd had enough and now determined to get out. Dave and I had both been brought up on London housing estates and neither of us had ever really had anything to call our own. During the boom years of the 1980s we decided to start up our own small business as a credit retailer or 'tally man'. We had a small van filled with bedding, quilts, covers, towels and household goods, like saucepans and dinner sets. We would go around the housing estates, knocking on doors, hoping to sell our wares. People would pay a small deposit for the goods they wanted and then we would call back one day each week for regular payments until the goods were paid for, rather like a mail order catalogue.

It was hard work. With two children, our second son was only a few days old when we started, a mortgage to pay on our little three-bedroomed house, interest rates rising all the time, and coping with the death of my dearly loved Nan, we were already struggling. But we were enthusiastic and supremely optimistic, so we went for it. We re-mortgaged the house and I took on an early morning cleaning job five days a week to help get us started. Our day would start with me walking out in the dark, in the wind and rain and all sorts of weather, and coming back to find John, our older son, who was two and a half at the time, already up and Dave warming a bottle and changing the baby's nappy, before leaving to spend the day finding customers. Most days he didn't get home until late evening.

Through our hard work, the business grew bigger quicker than we had anticipated, and pretty soon my mother was looking after the boys while I worked during the day as well. Five days a week turned into seven days a week, ten hours a day turned into fourteen hours a day. Coping with the accounts, buying and selling stock for a business which now had between five and six hundred customers, as well as looking after the boys, began to take its toll. We barely had time to say good morning or good night to each other before it was time to start all over again. We tried employing people but that only seemed to cause more problems. Something would always go wrong. They'd be rude to the customers, or run off with the takings or the stock. So we learned the hard way and stayed on our own.

It took us two years to get the business running well, but because we ploughed most of the profits back into the business we never seemed to benefit from our efforts. The larger the business became the harder we had to work. Then one night our van was stolen with all the stock in it. The insurance cover expired each evening at 9.00 pm because to have it on cover twenty four hours a day in the area we lived and worked meant very high premiums we just couldn't afford. I suppose with hindsight the way things turned out we should have paid it because by the time we had replaced everything our overdraft was up to its limit. Then a few weeks later, the same thing happened again, and then again; so each night we had to take it in turns to watch the van. I would wake Dave and he would take his turn for a couple of hours and then he would wake me and so on until daylight. We ended up with about four hours sleep each a night. The van itself was only worth £500, an old Y registered transit. We had a new alarm fitted with wires running everywhere, costing £1,000, which if set off would shout out repeatedly,

"ATTENTION, ATTENTION, THEFT IN PROGRESS," along with a horrid screeching sound. Once the wind set it off and in the dead of night it sounded as if the end of the world was coming. It caused a hell of a stir with the neighbours and the local police.

Around this time John started school. Well over five hundred children attended and John complained he was bored, there were so many children in his class his teacher had minimal time for them and held very little control. The school generally left a lot to be desired.

Along with the repeated attempts to steal our van, the final straw came when the Government decided to increase Value Added Tax. We felt we were working our fingers to the bone for nothing. We were always tired, there was hardly any time for each other or for the children. We didn't feel like a family any more. So we sat down and discussed it properly for the first time in ages and both agreed that we could not go on like this any longer. What we really wanted was to get out of London and start a new life somewhere in the country. So next morning I rang estate agents in Sussex, Kent, Norfolk, Somerset and Essex. The search was on - we had to get out. Every weekend from then on we set off on our travels, full of hope that we would find our dream cottage. But nothing that we looked at was in our price range or remotely like a cottage. However, on our travels we did find loads of car boot sales and we bought all sorts of bits and pieces to put away in the wardrobe for our cottage. This dream of ours was becoming an obsession. If we didn't find a cottage soon we'd have to buy a bigger wardrobe. By the time we had acquired two old milk churns the wardrobe doors would not close. The search for the cottage was getting no easier and only causing more stress and downheartedness. All the miles we were travelling were just adding to our tiredness.

"How about looking in Devon and Cornwall?" I suggested one morning.

"Don't be silly. It's too far to travel for work," Dave replied.

"Well we could always go for weekends," I said. But I could see that Dave was not too keen.

Whilst looking at cottages within reach of London it was our intention to carry on our business much as before, but hopefully without the stress and problems incurred by living in the place. If we found a cottage in the west country it would be a second home and would of course involve considerable expense, two mortgages for a start and we were already finding it hard to meet the repayments on just the one. But if we rented it out as a holiday home and just spent the occasional weekend or even a weeks holiday there, then the rent would pay the mortgage. My head was buzzing with ideas - could it work, will it work? I convinced myself it would work.

I got my teeth into the idea and phoned some estate agents in Devon. The big recession was beginning to bite and there were bargains to be had. The next day there was so much literature from the estate agents that the postman had to knock on the door and deliver them by hand. There were several that caught my eye straight away. As Dave was at work, I took the liberty of lining up several to view at the weekend. Mum said she would have the boys so that we could view them in peace.

Dave was not struck by the idea but he eventually agreed to go along with it and by daybreak on the Saturday morning we were on the road to Devon. It was a lovely clear morning and once again we were full of anticipation. The drive down through Somerset and on towards Exeter was beautiful. We could feel our lungs breathing in the fresh air and the stress of London lifting. We drove to Okehampton where we had arranged to meet the first estate agent around 9.30am. He was already there waiting for us, with the keys of the first cottage in his hand. It was vacant and due to be auctioned in three weeks. Something inside made my heart boom with excitement and I had an inner feeling Devon was the place for us. The drive down made us realise how much we wanted to move out of London. We wanted to see the children enjoying the countryside, living where they could learn to trust the people around them and to be close to animals, and seeing the simple joys that life can give. We set off to view the first cottage, the estate agent leading the way, and as we drove off there seemed to be a whole new life in front of us.

The countryside seemed even lovelier as we drove through the narrow lanes. The views were wonderful as we kept looking out of the car windows to see if we could spot anything that looked remotely like the picture in the estate agent's literature. His car stopped and we quickly looked about to see where our cottage was, then we realised he had stopped to let a chicken cross the road and we both laughed. We couldn't believe we had just seen a chicken cross the road. In London you only heard jokes about it, and the only chickens around were dead and frozen, and in the supermarket freezer. Here was a real live chicken happily pecking away in the hedgerow, oblivious to the road and the cars.

We carried on down the winding lanes and I was beginning to think we would never get there, when the estate agent's car pulled over. We were there. The reality of the cottage went far beyond my expectations. There was a pair of old-fashioned white gates and a long higgledy-piggledy barn and the cottage itself, all freshly painted.

Dave seemed hypnotised. I couldn't get out of the car quickly enough. As the estate agent opened the door I nearly knocked him over in my eagerness to see inside. The front door opened straight into the living room which had old cob walls, none of them straight, each about two feet thick and painted cream. Dave went into the little room to the right and said straightaway,

"Sonya, come quick and look at this."

In this room there stood an old fireplace with its original lintel and a bread oven surrounded by stone work with a large alcove in the wall next to it. I could imagine a great log fire burning there on a cold day. I found myself saying all excitedly,

"This is it! This is the place we've been looking for!" I was rushing around all over the place, looking in all the corners, full of enthusiasm, and thinking silly things like where we would put the tree at Christmas.

I believe we had made up our minds there and then, and we hadn't even seen the rest of the cottage. The agent obviously realising he was more than halfway to a sale, showed us upstairs. There were only two bedrooms, but they were both large and the views were panoramic from each, rolling hills and fields with only one other cottage in sight. I was in love with this place, all on its own in the middle of the countryside. It was just waiting to be loved and to be a home for a family who would appreciate it. In my mind I was already housing all the cottagey furniture and contents of our bulging wardrobe back in our London home. I wanted to move in then and there, while the enthusiasm was about me. The bathroom was cold and modern and somewhat of a let-down. It had carpets hanging on the walls, but it didn't matter, we could always change that. The kitchen was also modern, but all it needed was a farmhouse table and chairs, dried flowers hanging from the walls, lots of warmth and the smell of home cooking and it would be perfect.

Looking out of the kitchen window we saw a field, and asked who owned it and whether we might have access to it. Rather surprised he replied that it came with the house, it was all together. Once again I was overcome with emotion and rushed out of the back door. Maybe I would be able to have the pony I had always wanted since I was a child. All sorts of ideas flew through my head: flower beds, vegetable patches..... Dave was his usual self and said nothing, but I knew him and I knew this was the place for us and that he was thinking the same. It was however above our price range and I also knew he was sitting back quietly and considering.

As we said goodbye to the estate agent I was thinking of the painted milkchurns and where I could put them in the cottage. I was also wondering how we could raise the money to buy it. But we still had six more to see, and they were more within our price range. We were both really taken by Bramble Cottage, but perhaps we would like one of the others just as much.

By early evening we had travelled from one end of Devon to the other and viewed all the cottages, but all bar one had their faults one way or another. One was too dark, one needed re-roofing, another would have to be almost rebuilt. There was really no doubt about it, Bramble Cottage was the property for us. Our original intention was to stay in Devon overnight but we decided to get back to London as soon as possible and get to work. The cottage was to be auctioned shortly and there was plenty to do if we were to buy before then.

2
Moving In

Next morning we were up bright and early. Even though it was Sunday I phoned the estate agent and put in an offer. It was accepted, as long as we could exchange contracts within ten days! I managed to get a solicitor and though I had never met him, I promised he could have a free holiday in the cottage if he worked flat out to get all the paperwork done before the deadline. We made an appointment with the Building Society who to our delight approved a second mortgage. Life was even more hectic, the phone was constantly ringing, even late at night, and my adrenalin was on constant flow. There was no way we could take time off work. Not only did we have our present commitments but we now needed extra money to pay all the bills from the solicitors and the surveyors, we just did not have time to think. Amazingly we managed to get everything done in time and within two weeks we were the owners of Bramble Cottage. We just could not believe it.

Now we had to prepare for the move and decide how to furnish our new home. At last we could empty the bulging wardrobe and we started loading all the things that we had been collecting for so long into the van we had hired in preparation for the next weekend. My heart was beating so fast I thought I might explode. Such a sense of achievement and joyful anticipation brought permanent smiles to our faces as big as Cheshire cats. We just could not wait to see the cottage again. By Friday night we had the van all loaded up and just about managed to close the shutter at the back. Mum agreed to have the boys again for the weekend and Dad had said that he would gladly come with us and help us move our bits and pieces in. That night I was so excited I hardly slept a wink, going over and over in my mind what we were going to unpack first, and where I was going to put everything. I tossed and turned all night and when finally daylight broke we were already washed and dressed. Within the hour we were on our way.

We picked up my Dad who was all ready in his working clothes, with his bag of tools and just as eager as we were. It took us longer than we had anticipated to drive down to Devon, the van being so loaded, but once we had picked up the keys, the sun started to shine and by early afternoon we had arrived at our cottage. As we pulled up we were greeted by several cows looking over the fence from the field next door. Dad looked around - his face was a picture.

"Is this it?" he asked.

"Yes," we said, and looking at it for the second time ourselves, we could hardly believe it either. Wild flowers were growing in the hedgerows and apart from the cows making noises that cows do there was not a sound to be heard.

"Blimey love, this is bloody lovely," Dad said, " I never dreamt it was anything like this."

When we opened the door it smelt empty, but homely, just as old and cosy as we remembered and not a single regret crossed our minds. It was all too much for words.

We very quickly made ourselves busy unloading and unpacking, fixing things up and fitting things together. Dad's tools certainly came in handy and by late evening much had been achieved and we all had a great feeling of satisfaction. Then we noticed the pitch-black outside, no street lights or houses, only open countryside. Once night fell there was only a large black space with which the imagination could run riot and a stunning silence. You took the noise for granted in London, there was never any quietness no matter where you went. Here it was so peaceful, but quite eerie and we were glad to shut the door and stay in our cosy lounge.

On Sunday we finished what we could, and although we were sad to leave, we knew that this little cottage was really ours, even if it hadn't completely sunk in yet. It was like a fairy-tale, to have something so precious when we were so young, and to have all our hard work count for something tangible in the end. But for now until next weekend we had to go back to London, to work, back to the stress of a life we hated so much, and back to watching the van each night

On the drive back to London my mind was racing over everything we needed to do. It was all so new to me. Sometimes in the winter storms we were told the electricity would be cut off for days and so a gas cooker or Rayburn was needed.

Before we could light the fire we needed to sweep the chimney and buy a grate and keep a big pile of logs stacked in the barn. It was all so exciting. Something else I had never heard of before was the septic tank, this I learned would have to be pumped out when full.

No doubt some people would say we were out of our minds getting this little place in the middle of nowhere, giving up central heating, shag pile carpets, fast cars and discos. But we were really happy despite the mortgages, the overdraft and the prospect of having to work harder than ever to meet our financial commitments. As we approached London the traffic became heavier and there was not a tractor to be seen. We could feel the stress returning with the noise, the pollution and drivers getting irate with each other. Ninety minutes earlier we had been driving along country lanes and now we were at a standstill in another traffic jam. Gone was the smell of the fresh air and logs burning. Now it was exhaust fumes. Against the din of cars revving, stereos blaring, even dogs fighting, my Dad remarked,

"Well mate, it's back to the old grindstone again."

We had promised to take the boys to Devon the following weekend and as the week went by they became more and more excited. So were we. Friday night came at last and we set off in the van as soon as we had finished work. Our eyes were stinging with tiredness and we felt like stopping and having a sleep, but just then a badger ran across the road in front of us. We had never seen a real live badger before. For the rest of the journey we talked and talked about everything, something we hadn't done for months. We were all together again. We arrived at Bramble Cottage about two in the morning. The boys were frightened of the pitch black dark but once inside the cottage they were running excitedly from one room to another. Eventually we got them to sleep and went to bed ourselves. The cottage is old, about four hundred years old, and at night there were all kinds of strange noises we weren't used to.

In the morning we went to the post office in the nearby village and introduced ourselves to the local post master. We explained that we wanted to rent the cottage out for holiday lets to help pay the mortgage, and we needed somebody to look after it for us. He was very helpful and told us that he knew of somebody who might be able to help us out. Later that afternoon a lady came to the door,

"I hear you are looking for a sort of caretaker come cleaner."

We couldn't believe our luck. Her name was Hazel and she seemed really nice. We sat for ages talking about the people in the area and the way of life. Her husband Lester was a plumber and they lived just ten minutes walk away. After a couple of hours I felt as if I had known her for ages. I liked her. She could start as soon as we got our first booking. It was great to be able to sit and chat like friends

The next problem was outside. The grass and hedges were very overgrown and we had no way of cutting them back. Hazel suggested asking George, a farmer who lived up the lane. So on Sunday morning we went along to the farm and introduced ourselves. It was an old farm where he lived with his wife Esther, their daughter Shirley and son Trevor, and hundreds of animals. Everywhere you looked there were cows, sheep, horses, cats, dogs, ferrets and lots of ducks, chickens and cockerels all seemingly living as they pleased.

They made us very welcome in their farmhouse which was old and full of character, with the smell of cooking mingling with the warmth of the open fire. We explained our problem and George said that he would cut our grass but couldn't do the hedges because for one thing it was the wrong time of the year, and anyhow he didn't possess a hedgecutter, but his nephew would cut them back in the autumn when he trimmed his own.

After that we had to say our thank-you's and goodbyes and go back to Bramble Cottage to lock up before returning to London again ready for next week's work and school. It was such a quick change in such a short space of time - the Devon way of life to the London way of life!

It was during the next week back in London that I took our first holiday booking for the cottage, a middle-aged couple wanted it for the next weekend. Two days later the phone rang again and it was for another booking. This was the beginning of our next unexpected problem; too many bookings. The phone kept ringing and the bookings kept coming in, and it wasn't long before the whole of the summer was fully booked, and Hazel was being kept really busy every Saturday morning as the holiday change-overs took place.

The weather was lovely that summer, but back in London we were stuck in our rut of working non-stop with no time to get away. I was beginning to wonder where all the excitement had gone. We never saw our cottage for months. I began to resent the holiday-makers even though I knew they were helping to pay for it. They were staying in my cottage, sleeping in my bed, drinking out of my cups, sitting in my field, not knowing what they looked like, and wondering if they were leaving the place tidy or not. I wished that I could unbook just one weekend and go down there and make sure everything was alright. I wanted to be in Devon smelling the fresh air not in smelly London. But the cottage was booked until Christmas and that was that. The next time that we would be in our dream cottage would be Christmas Eve. All I could do was talk to Hazel each weekend and ask if every thing in the cottage was safe and sound. Each time we were lucky, but each time I felt so powerless and felt such a strong urge to go down to Devon. I even contemplated renting a caravan nearby for a weekend so that we could at least see the cottage but I quickly dismissed that idea.

Then we had a stroke of luck. I had a phone call early one morning from a very apologetic lady who told me that her dog had been taken ill and she would be unable to take her holiday in our cottage. She realised that it was short notice but had rung me early to give me what little notice there was to re-book it. I told her I was very sorry to hear about her dog, but not to worry as I knew a family who would gladly take the cottage at short notice.

"Yes, Yes, Yes!" I cried as I put down the phone.

Next weekend the cottage was to be ours, all ours. We could see it again for only the third time since we bought it.

Arriving at Bramble Cottage again everything seemed just as we had left it four months ago. It was such a relief to find it looking just the same, the grass kept down and the house looking clean and tidy. The bedroom looked cosier than ever with the pretty linen freshly washed and ironed, and the pretty curtains hanging at the windows. It was as if nobody had been in there at all.

Soon we were sitting in the sun enjoying a cup of tea and a sandwich, watching the boys playing in the field behind the cottage. Shouting with excitement they chased around playing hide and seek, already completely at home, even Judy our old dog took on a new lease of life exploring her new territory. For the first time in months were able to sit back and relax, it was bliss.

It didn't take long to get the boys settled that night, they were tired with all the travelling and excitement. Dave and I were just settling ourselves down for the night when there was a tap at the door.

"Got the kettle on?" came a cheerful voice, it was Hazel.

"You haven't walked down on your own in the dark, have you?" I asked her, for it was pitch black outside.

"Well I haven't flown," she said laughing, it didn't seem to bother her, "there's no-one about down here, this isn't London you know."

But the thought still frightened me, I didn't fancy walking around these lanes in the dark with no street lights. We started chatting and Hazel told us about the people who owned the farms and cottages around us. It turned out that Hazel's auntie and uncle had lived in our cottage for many years until they died, her uncle had been a carpenter and had done most of his work in the cob barn. After their deaths the cottage was sold to a Mr Parsonson who spent a considerable sum of money putting in a new kitchen and a new bathroom and making other improvements. He was the man from whom we purchased the cottage, although we actually never met him. It made me think of all the people who may have lived in our little cottage. From the conversation it seemed that many of the people around here were related and we wondered if they found it sad to see one of their cottages being bought by a family from London.

I asked Hazel where the nearest school was.

"Don't you know?" she said laughing, "It's the building at the back, just two fields over." Although very small the school had over fifty pupils, a swimming pool, computers and even a little garden. There were two teachers and a headmaster who also took lessons, a typical village school according to Hazel. I thought of John's school back in London. I never imagined little village schools like this existed anymore.

That night we lay listening to the gentle stillness, recalling all the things we had talked about during the evening. It just didn't seem right that we had to go back to London the very next day. I so wanted to suggest staying another week, as we knew the cottage would be empty. It seemed so sad, the boys were so happy here and it was almost as if they had never been anywhere else. Next morning we tried not to think about London and enjoyed a good tramp through the countryside, but finally departure time came. We snatched a few more minutes in the garden with a cup of tea before setting off. It was so beautiful. Dave knew what I was thinking and came over and put his arm around me.

" Living down here would be like one continuous holiday, just us and the kids and Judy, no matter we wouldn't have much money Sonya, if only we could find some kind of work down here." With such a large mortgage to support it looked as if we would just have to keep our little cottage for holidays, our place of escape, at least for a few years yet, but as we headed back for London I could not help thinking about it.

3
Our First Christmas in Devon

Christmas time was approaching and it was always a busy time for our business as customers were wanting to buy their presents. This year we added toys to our stock and they were selling very well. However, as customers were paying for them by weekly instalments it meant that our purchasing bills were astronomical. We spent thousands of pounds on stock but still needed more to meet demand. It was a real struggle and in a way we were victims of our own success. We were still having to watch the van at night, get up early and work sixteen hours a day. We were both constantly tired, and with no time to talk to the boys they were suffering too. So come December 23rd it was a great relief to load up the van with everything we would need for Christmas, including a large turkey and the biggest Christmas tree you have ever seen, and set off for Devon. My Mother and her husband Frank were coming down on Christmas Eve to spend the holiday with us, they had never seen the cottage before. Just knowing that we could relax for two whole weeks was like winning the lottery.

It was so lovely to see the countryside again although different in the winter, but just as beautiful and the holly bush outside our gates was covered in berries. There was another surprise waiting for Dave when he went inside the cottage, for I had secretly arranged with Hazel that her husband Lester should put up some beams in the living room.

"Hazel's been in here with the pledge," Dave called out when he opened the door. Then when he looked up his face was a picture. The beams were marvellous, the wood was very old and they made the room feel even cosier than before and added so much character. I'd been sending little sums of money down to Hazel that I'd saved out of the family allowance and the housekeeping to pay for the alterations; it had been a squeeze but it was really worth it.

After we unpacked and set the Christmas tree in the pot ready for decorating, we went to see if the fire grate we were having made was ready yet. Hazel had organised a large pile of logs for us and we wanted to see a fire blazing in the fireplace. George was out on the farm but we found Esther in the milking shed with her Friesians. They all had names with 'Rose' in them, Big Rose, Little Rose, Ann Rose and so on. As one went out of the milking shed, Esther would call another by name and in it would come. Amazingly they answered to all their names. We watched the milking for a while and then went in to a large mug of tea each and warmed ourselves around the Aga. Their Christmas decorations were all up and the Christmas cake took pride of place on the sideboard. Just then George walked in.

"Hello, how be then?" he called out and gave us all big hugs. It was lovely to be made so welcome. Finally we got round to having a look at the fire grate he had made for us. It was perfect, you would never be able to buy one like it. It was heavy and had lots of fancy iron work, it must have taken him hours to make. One thing puzzled me, there was a little round plate on a wrought iron arm that swivelled either over or away from the fire. When I asked him what it was for he gave me a smile with the usual twinkle in his eye and said,

"That my dear is to put your cup of tea on to keep it warm." We were over the moon with the grate but it looked very expensive.

"How much do I owe you George?"

"Well try it out first and see if you like it."

We had quite a struggle getting it through the front door but finally it sat in the fire place and looked as though it had been there for years. I hung the horse brasses that I had brought with me while Dave made the fire up and the boys brought in some logs.The fire filled the room with the homely smell only a log fire can give. We decorated the Christmas tree and the tension of the previous weeks lifted as we all started to relax.

Even though we knew very few of the people who lived around us we still received several Christmas cards which was so typical of the thoughtfulness and kindness of the locals. The boys put them up and with the decorations the room soon looked wonderful.

Next day my Mum, Frank and Grandad arrived, a bit late as they had managed to get lost in the lanes. They were overwhelmed by the beauty of the countryside and our delightful Bramble Cottage. The boys were so excited, they wanted to show them everything at once. The rest of the day passed in happy chaos as we prepared for Christmas Day. We had brought with us an inflatable six foot Father Christmas that we fetched from the warehouse in London and Dave and Frank were nominated to blow him up. Their enthusiasm was great at first but as the thing got bigger and bigger we could hardly see them behind it. It was a hilarious sight as they struggled to inflate it and it slowly filled the whole kitchen, pinning Frank to the back door. Mum and me were trying to wipe away the tears of laughter when the boys came in to see what all the commotion was about, their eyes widened in disbelief when they saw him and when they tried to cuddle him, but he was far too big. He was also too big for the house so we put him in the porch where he became a great local attraction. Some people passing in their cars even stopped and took a photo of him!

It was a lovely Christmas. Although the weather was atrocious we were happy and snug in the cottage, altogether round the log fire, well-fed and well warm. After a week Mum, Frank and Grandad left to go home but we still had another week to enjoy ourselves. Each morning after a hearty breakfast we'd pull on our wellies and have tramp about our field and the surrounding countryside and country lanes. We always found something new, something to surprise us. We were settling into this way of life perfectly. We spent New Year's Eve on our own and when midnight struck we saw the New Year in standing in the back garden looking up at the stars wondering what the next twelve months would bring. I knew what I wanted it to bring and I think it was then my mind was made up.

The first day of the New Year was wet and blustery, we walked up to George and Esther's farm, and as usual were made very welcome. All the family, except Esther, were suffering from the celebrations of the night before. They'd left leaving the local pub until very late and when checking a sheep that was lambing found her in difficulty, and hadn't got to bed until gone four that morning. They then had to get up early to go to market. They were all so busy I asked George's daughter Shirley if there was anything I could do. She was making up a bottle of milk to feed the lambs and she promptly thanked me and handed me a feed bottle. We went into the old barn and turned over a bale of hay on which to sit while we fed the lambs on our laps. They were only a few hours old and did not seem to mind us at all while they sucked eagerly on the bottles.

Shirley explained that she and George were in a hurry to see the local Hunt that was gathering at the pub, and asked us along. I'm not a hunt supporter but realised that hunting was part of country life and that foxes were a real problem to the local farmers and I knew what I would want to do to a fox if it had killed any of my chickens. The Hunt looked spectacular, the riders in their smart jackets and their beautifully turned out horses waiting for the off. The bugle sounded and the Hunt Master led with the beagles and other riders following, with more supporters following on foot. I hadn't realised that it was such a big event especially with the weather so bad. Dave took the boys back to the cottage but I stayed on with Shirley. Three hours later we came home, wet, freezing cold and having had no glimpse whatsoever of anything that remotely resembled a fox. I really wondered what I was doing.

The wet holiday period brought us another problem, although we had soak-aways, our soak-away was just not soaking away! The cottage lies just a little lower than the field behind so the water was flowing back downhill all around the cottage. George contacted another farmer, Steve, who said that he would come and have a look. He came with his tractor and all the necessary equipment to suck up the water into a big tank, but as fast as he was emptying the soak-away it was filling straight up again. After he'd been at it for two or three hours without much success he suggested we get a digger to dig a trench to drain the water away, but it was too late in the day for that now. Later that evening George came by with another farmer, Rupert, to look at what could be done, and by now because of the heavy rain, the water was coming up through a crack in our living room floor and soaking the carpet. George and Rupert spent a long time out in the field in the pouring rain assessing the problem. They concluded that we would have to get a JCB in to dig a trench. Even with experts on the scene it turned out to be a complicated job. We were lucky to get a digger the next day from Holsworthy and the work began digging spurs across our field and laying pipes to drain the water away. Seeing our green field turned into a muddy heap was heartbreaking but we knew it had to be done. The boys thought it was fantastic. The weather was still appalling, with winds gusting 95 mph and a mixture of sleet, hale and snow seemingly blowing from all directions. This didn't put the boys off though.

"Oh no you don't, you come back in!" I shouted as I caught them putting on their boots and sneaking out the back door.

"We want to help Dad," they chorused. But something told me that Dave would get the job done a lot quicker without their help and they had to be content to sit and watch the digger from the window, along with Judy in the dry. In the meantime, Rupert, the chief supervisor as I had fondly named him, came round to say that his wife Joy would be very pleased to meet us if we wanted to pop round sometime. They lived in the dairy farm just up the road beyond the thatched cottage. I offered him a cup of tea and as he settled himself into the rocking chair saying that he couldn't stay long as he had lots of jobs to do at home, he regaled us with all the local scandal and finally left over an hour later. He looked out of the window to where the two men were still working and struggling against the elements.

"They're doing a good job, a couple of hours and they'll be nearly finished, you won't even know they've been there." I had to laugh, was he seeing the same field as me? There was now just one big mountain of wet running clay and soil, JCB tyre marks all over the place and men sloshing around in the mud.

Rupert went home and after putting on my waterproofs I popped out with two mugs of tea. The wind and rain were blowing me sideways and I could hardly catch my breath. Chris the digger driver, was looking worried, water was gushing everywhere and he thought we might have a burst water main under the cottage somewhere. He had never seen anything like this in all the years he had been doing drainage work - why do workmen always say that? We were due to go home two days later so we had to press on. Eventually all the pipes were laid and come early evening all the drainage ditches were filled, and to cap it all a pale evening sun came out. At last the job was done and with the work completed the field looked more like its old self. Come the spring grass I was sure everything would be fine.

We managed to squeeze in a visit to Rupert and Joy before returning to London and was surprised to find such a smart farm, everything was so clean, even the two sheepdogs who came to greet us so warmly with tails wagging. My impression of Rupert was of someone who would happily just let things be but I couldn't have been more wrong. The farmhouse was spacious and stylish and there was an extension where their son Dave, his wife and their twelve months old son lived. Joy's mum also lived with them, she was ninety six years old and still quite strong. We sat chatting for a while over the customary cup of tea and before we left Rupert showed us the trophies he'd won over the years with his cattle. We left clutching a pot of home-made clotted cream and as we drove back to Bramble Cottage we felt so contented that it just did not seem possible that tomorrow we would be back in London.

We'd not been back at the cottage for more than half an hour when Hazel popped in to ask whether the boys would like to go to the Sunday School party. Of course little ears heard mention of jelly and ice cream and how could we say no. So later that afternoon we drove up to Hazels, the church hall was next door and about twenty excited children were already there. When we entered it was like stepping back to the 1930s. All the furnishings and fittings were pre-war and I honestly couldn't remember seeing anything quite like it before. John settled down with the other children straight away but Ricky wasn't so sure, he was still too young to appreciate it all. The Sunday School teacher introduced herself and said the boys would always be welcome. Here we were, once again experiencing first hand the genuine warmth and affection of the locals towards a family from miles away, of whom they knew so little and yet were prepared to offer so much. I thought of some of our friends back in London who upon hearing of our intentions to buy a place in Devon said,

"Oh you won't like it down there - they don't accept people from our part of the world," or words to that effect.

Of course we were 'incomers' and very much aware of it, but we were never made to feel unwelcome or not wanted, always quite the opposite. When we picked John up later he told us about his new friends and again how friendly everyone was.

It was with heavy hearts that next day we took down the Christmas tree and packed away all the decorations, and prepared for our drive back to the capital. We had to clean the cottage thoroughly in case we could not get down again before the holiday-makers started to arrive. On reflection it's strange how much we have changed. Several years ago I would never have dreamed of having a holiday in the countryside, let alone wanting to live there, I would have thought it was far too quiet and dull, but since having a family my ambitions have changed and now to be with Dave and the boys enjoying the peace and beauty of the countryside together is something I will settle for. I was so proud of what we had achieved and so glad that we had a goal in life we thought worth aiming for, not solely competing in the cut-throat lifestyle of London.

Once back however, we soon fell into the old routine, the phone started ringing as soon as we got into the house, the work began piling up and before the week was out we seemed tired out and finding it impossible to have enough time for the boys. I felt so guilty but we had to keep working as hard as we could.

We'd received no holiday bookings for the rest of January and February and in the middle of February Hazel phoned to say they'd had six inches of snow and Lester was unable to get to work, and the school was closed because there was no heating. I knew it would be cold but I really wanted to see our cottage and the fields under a carpet of snow.

I wasn't to be disappointed, it was the weekend and within a few hours we were on our way, once again Dave and the boys needed no persuasion. We began to see traces of snow the closer we came to Devon and by the time we had reached Okehampton it was thick everywhere. We wondered what the cottage was going to be like after five weeks of standing empty. The sheep and cows in the fields were pulling greedily at their hay bales and the trees and hedges were drooping with the weight of the snow. It was breathtakingly beautiful - all the farmhouses and outbuildings covered with snow and the lights twinkling in the half darkness, it was just like a Christmas card scene. By the time we arrived at Bramble Cottage it was pitch black and far too dark for the boys to make their first snowman, they would have to wait till morning. Although the cottage was very cold and our teeth were chattering it was still welcoming and soon we had a good fire roaring in the grate. After a quick supper we happily went to bed cuddling our hot water bottles.

Next morning we peeped out of the windows, snow everywhere! We all ate a big breakfast and put on three layers of clothing. I sneaked out first and took some photographs of the field without any footprints on it, all the trees and surrounding fields were covered in crisp white snow, not a car or a tractor in sight.

We all joined in building the biggest snowman you ever saw. Judy was barking and digging in the snow, she produced her cracker I'd given her at Christmas which she had obviously left in the field. Just as I put the last bit of snow on the snowman his head fell off. Laughing we all helped rebuild him and took another photo for the family album, we were very proud of our first ever snowman with his stick arms and bucket head.

When calling on George and Esther we received our customary genuine welcome; Esther had put up a bird table outside the kitchen window and we all watched a robin picking up the crumbs for his breakfast, we hadn't seen many robins before, probably because we had been too busy to notice them. We were learning fast some of the simplest things in life are often the best.

We drove into Bideford through snowy lanes but in Bideford itself there was no trace of snow. Being a coastal town the sea air had prevented it from laying. The town was very quiet but we found a chippy open which served our appetites and after an hour or so drove slowly back to the cottage. Sitting by the fire that evening I asked Dave when and if he thought it would be possible to move to Devon permanently.

"I don't know," he replied, "but I'm sick and tired of London, I wish we didn't have to go back this time - one day hopefully." We were sinking into depression just thinking about having to go back.

The next morning while we were still lying in bed, we were startled by something on the roof outside. It was a barn owl. I jumped out of bed to get my camera but his beady eyes had spotted something and he was off. It was a beautiful sight to see his wings stretch out as he flew over the hedge, hover for a second and then dive for whatever it was he had seen, a mouse or something, and then fly off gracefully towards the woods. It was all over in seconds but the memory will stay with me for ever.

We were all very quiet on the journey back to London. We'd made the most of our short break and didn't really want to go back this time, we wanted to stay at Bramble Cottage. We talked it through suggesting this and that but the fact remained there were very few jobs in Devon. What could we do? I had learned through hard experience that if you really want something you have to go out and get it, don't just talk about it. I made up my mind to do just that.

Once back in London I sought out a friend who had a large contract with a firm that had credit retail rounds like ours all over the country. I also discussed it with my brother who was also in the same line of business. Both suggested it might be worth having a look around Devon to see if it might be feasible to start up a similar business down there. My brother said he would come down and help us canvass the area and build up the business.

However, what could we do with the existing business we had in London. The recession held everything in a tight grip and businesses were closing down daily, and I knew that nobody would have the money to buy us out. Selling our house would be another problem, there were already three up for sale in our street that had attracted precious little interest for a year or more. The property market was extremely quiet and we were still paying off a huge overdraft. With interest rates at an all time high we could only just cover the interest payments never mind pay off some of the capital. It was ridiculous to consider moving, we would be risking everything.

In the meantime I advertised Bramble Cottage again for holiday lets in order to raise some money that would help pay the mortgage, but I only wanted to let it for the next three months in case our position might change. Dave thought I'd taken leave of my senses not to be taking bookings for the whole summer when we needed the money so much. Maybe I had and it was certainly a big worry hanging over our heads but I just had this feeling it was the right thing to do.

All through February and March I spent any spare time decorating the house just in case it went on the market. I cleaned out all the rubbish so that it was spotlessly clean the whole time. Any loose change I put in a jar to put towards the solicitor's bill. I knew that as a family we belonged in our little cottage in Devon away from the aggravation of the city and I was going to do everything and anything within my powers to make it happen.

We visited Devon several times during those months, still driving down in our old transit van and each time taking with us more furniture and bits and pieces. On one occasion my father came with us to help Dave renew some guttering. Along with the guttering we had a Welsh Dresser, cleaning buckets and a deckchair on which I had to sit for the whole journey with Ricky on my lap. He fell asleep and prevented me moving anymore than resting my legs on a step ladder. We arrived at 2.30 in the morning, my legs were by now badly cramped and everyone's patience was stretched to the limit, but even then in the pitch black the cottage was as welcoming as ever. It really felt like arriving home.

Next morning the sun was shining brilliantly and as I looked out of the window my heart lifted. Where a few weeks ago there had been thick snow there were now primroses and crocuses flowering in their hundreds, and the hazel tree next to the cob barn was covered in catkins. For several minutes I was overwhelmed by a feeling of utter contentment and I knew our permanent move to Devon was soon to become a reality.

Back in London our minds were constantly in Devon.

"Are we going to Devon this weekend?" the boys would ask.

"We'll try," I would answer.

Towards the end of March someone phoned to ask if they might rent the cottage for the following weekend. We needed the money so had to say yes and I phoned Hazel to let her know. Later that evening Hazel rang back. Lester had seen a jackdaw looking at him from one of our bedroom windows as he had driven past our cottage. He'd had no time to stop then but told Hazel upon his return home. When she opened the door of the cottage she found the place turned upside down! Dried flowers and ornaments were all over the floor and each room was a total shambles. Upstairs she found two dead jackdaws and one very much still alive and bird's mess everywhere. They'd even been in the bathroom but at least one bird had the decency to use the toilet! What a good job Lester had seen the jackdaw that morning, Hazel had just enough time to clean up all the mess before the holiday makers arrived.

Next weekend we decided to go down and fit a cowl on the chimney to stop the birds getting in again. Lester helped Dave while Hazel and I were able to have a chat, I thanked her for all the hard work she had done getting the cottage to rights. The holiday-makers had been none the wiser, and even remarked on how clean they found the cottage.

We went to the local garden centre where we purchased several shrubs and roses and an apple tree for the far end of the field. Once back at the cottage we had great fun planning where to plant the tree. After much debate we decided on the perfect spot and Dave duly conducted the planting, but on looking out of the upstairs window next morning realised it was in completely the wrong place, as it would block the view as it grew bigger and that would never do. So for the second time Dave conducted a planting ceremony, but this time it was raining hard and blowing a gale. He was not amused!

The spring flowers were now starting to bloom and the countryside had that lovely fresh green appearance about it you only get in these months. We'd even seen badgers in the fields and spent several minutes watching the baby rabbits play under the hedgerows, which in turn were hiding the nests of blackbirds, thrushes and other wild birds. It was all so beautiful and all so far removed from London, but for the moment we had to return in order to earn the money to pay for our Bramble Cottage. Back to watching the van all night and working all hours. One morning as John was getting ready for school he asked,

"When are we going to put this house up for sale mum, and move down to Devon?"

"Today, I'll do it today," I answered.

4
On The Move - For Good

"This is the prettiest house in the street," said the estate agent, "but with the current state of the market it may still take a year or more to sell."

"Thanks very much," I muttered under my breath. I had half been expecting that, but I didn't want to hear it. I was well aware some people who had their houses up for sale down our street had not even had one single person to view. However, we put ours on the market at a price a little lower than the others and hoped for the best. We might face a long wait but at least the decision was taken and the wheels were in motion. An hour later the phone rang, the estate agent had a lady with him who wanted to view the house right away.

"Can she come straight over?"

I couldn't believe it, and told myself not to get too excited, she might just be nosey, I had to prepare myself for a disappointment. I needn't have worried, she stayed the whole afternoon talking non-stop about the house. She was a widow with one daughter and said the house was exactly what they were looking for. She put in an offer there and then, which I had no hesitation in accepting. We arranged that we would both inform the estate agent which for my part I did as soon as she was out of the door; he was as surprised as me.

When Dave came home from work that evening I couldn't tell him the news quick enough, I was so excited. When our jubilation subsided the reality of the situation began to take over, there were so many things to see to and arrangements to be made. It was going to be a real headache, but at least the first hurdle was cleared. First thing next morning I rang my brother John to confirm he would still come down to Devon and help us canvass customers for the credit retail business we intended to start up. Although very busy himself he said he would come down as soon as we needed him and bring his friend Mac to help as well. I also made another phone call to a long-time friend who was in the same business as us and although we hadn't spoken for probably a couple of years I asked him if he would like to buy any or all of our existing business in London.

It was all happening so quickly. The country was in the middle of a recession and like many other businesses we ran on an overdraft and had more debts than we felt comfortable with. We really had to keep working right up to the time of the move, but the next afternoon I said to Dave,

"How about picking John up from school and going down to Devon for the night? We could use the excuse that we have to look around the housing estates for future business potential."

"Not a chance, we've got to carry on working."

Within the hour we had loaded some belongings on the van and were waiting for John outside his school. The house was beginning to look bare now but to know that we were so close to living in Devon was fantastic. Soon we left the noise of London behind us and were once again appreciating the beautiful countryside . When we arrived the sun was low in the sky and long shadows danced across the hills.

We had a good look around some of the housing estates of Launceston and Bodmin but until we had physically canvassed them we wouldn't know just how much business they would generate. However, first impressions were encouraging. I longed for the mornings when I would be driving to work along the country lanes instead of through London traffic jams. We followed the same routine for the next few weekends, quick runs down to Devon and back, until our house in London was just about empty. The solicitors were still going about their business, it seemed to be taking for ever. One evening we'd just sat down by the fire in the cottage having got the boys off to bed when Judy started barking excitedly. We let her out and followed to investigate, it was pitch black outside.

"Can you see anything?" We couldn't even see Judy but she was still barking away, clearly trying to tell us something or somebody was about. Then suddenly we heard a loud 'MOO' and we just about jumped out of our skins. A cow had wandered into our field from next door and was standing outside the kitchen window; we could just about make out the white bits of what I later learned was a Friesian - Friesians being black and white.

Each time we travelled down to Devon I brought all sorts of cottage plants - phlox, carnations, lupins, stocks and foxgloves, so that by the time we moved in the garden would be looking really pretty.

On one of our visits we popped into the local school and spoke to the headmaster. Trying to keep our business going in London and canvass for new business in Devon meant that for a few weeks we thought we might have to divide our time between London and Devon. The headmaster was very pleasant and he agreed to let John do a three-day week for as long as necessary. He appreciated our position and was happy to go along with it. It was certainly a lovely school, with a swimming pool, football pitch and its own garden. We were sure that John and later Ricky, would be very happy there. We were invited for a cup of coffee and the teachers and secretary came to meet us in the classroom while the children worked. I have never seen such well-behaved happy children; it was totally different to John's London school.

On another occasion I had to visit the local hospital in Barnstaple to get my eye seen to, and once again what a difference! I had already been to a hospital in London after managing to get some scouring pad in my eye, (don't ask me how I managed it) which was causing me some considerable discomfort. There I had to wait two and a half hours to be seen and the hospital was really mucky, the walls were covered with graffiti and the doctors were so busy I felt as if I was on a conveyer belt. But in Barnstaple the hospital was spotless, I only had to wait five minutes and the doctors had more time for the patients. Soon my eye was a great deal better and I was able to see with both eyes again. I appreciated seeing the roses and the honeysuckle beginning to grow over the trellis we had nailed to the wall of the cottage, and I knew I would never take my eyesight for granted again.

After the weekend we arrived back in London to find a letter from the solicitors waiting for us saying that all parties were ready to exchange contracts. We were very excited as it had come a lot sooner than expected. We wanted to celebrate but with our finances being so tight we made do with a plate of ham sandwiches and mugs of tea.

Now we really had to get our business affairs sorted out. I phoned my friend once again and he was quite happy to buy one of our credit retail rounds from us, and the very next day Dave had a real stroke of luck. He'd met a chap who was willing to buy the rest of the business. There must be a catch I thought when Dave told me, but apparently not, he and this man had actually been about to knock on the same door and they started talking. The man explained that he was just starting up and looking for more customers. Dave told him we were just leaving and were trying to sell off our rounds, so there and then the man agreed to buy off the remaining rounds, debts and all!

Next day I rang our solicitor and the estate agents, they confirmed everybody was ready to move so we signed our contracts ready for completion the following week. It was a hectic week, we went up to our overdraft limit buying stock for our new credit rounds in Devon and the stockist agreed to deliver them for us . My brother John and his pal Mac agreed to travel down on Monday, if we moved over the weekend, and start canvassing straight away. We hired a large van as our old transit was full of stock, and loaded up the rest of our furniture. Once again we were so excited and on Saturday 25th May 1991 we were ready to leave London for good, no regrets only happiness and excitement for the future. Only that morning I had been round the markets buying vegetables and chatting with the barrow boys I had known for years, but nobody knew that we were leaving in a few hours time. I'd shared a lot of laughs with these people over the years and made some good friends, but London was changing and not for the better. At one time people would stick up for each other and any disagreements were quickly resolved, everybody knew one another. But it was changing fast now, a lot of the Londoners were moving out and strangers were moving in with their greed and their aggression.

I pulled the door hard shut for the last time, and as we drove off down the road looked straight ahead - I was determined not to look back. This was the first day of the rest of our lives and I only wanted to look forward.

It was a gloriously sunny day and we all felt so happy as we made our way along the M4, M5 and finally the A30 to Okehampton, where we turned off for the final few miles along Devon's lanes. When we reached Bramble Cottage there was a welcome card from each of Hazel's children waiting for us on the dining table. Steven had written to John, 'I promise I will look after you at school.'

Next morning we were wakened by a cockerel! Not a real one, just the alarm clock shaped like a cockerel that we had bought back in London. It wasn't as good as the real thing but it did its job and Dave got up to take the hired van back to London and return in our transit van. It was another beautiful day and Judy, the boys and myself spent the whole day unpacking bits and pieces and then weeding the garden. We were relieved to welcome Dave home that evening with our own van, he was looking happier and more relaxed than I'd seen him for ages. It was a strange feeling, we could not really believe that we were in Devon full time, that we wouldn't have to pack up and drive the long journey back to London. We kept expecting it to disappear - like a dream that was just about to end, it was going to take a while to sink in.

Mac and my brother couldn't get down until Wednesday so we had a completely free day on Tuesday. We heard there was a cattle and poultry market in Hatherleigh on a Tuesday so we drove over to have a look. It was easy to find, tractors, cattle lorries and people everywhere, we bought some onions from one of the stalls and then went over to the livestock section. Ducks, chickens, geese, rabbits and all sorts were up for auction. I found myself bidding for four ducks, Dave looked astonished.

"£1.20, £1.50, £1.80, the bid is against you madam," the auctioneer shouted out.

I looked up and realised he was looking at me! I nodded not really knowing what he meant.

"Any advance on £2, £2 and going..." Bang, down went the hammer. "Name, madam?" he asked. I was too embarrassed to shout out O'Donoghue, there were so many people looking at me , so I shouted 'Jones', my face was as red as a beetroot.

"We've just bought four ducks," I said to Dave.

"Correction, you've just bought four ducks. Where are we going to put them? What are we going to feed them? I can't go out buying them fish every day. Whatever made you go and do that?"

"I just thought they looked nice," I replied feebly. A farmer told me where to go and pay, it turned out to be 50p each £2 for the four, so I thought I'd got a bargain. We managed to get a box to put them in and carried them proudly over to our van. Dave wasn't saying much but I could tell he didn't really mind, he would be fine once we had given them some names. On the way home we decided to pop into George's farm to see if we could get some advice on duck management.

"You've only been moved in for two days," George laughed when I told him what I'd just done, "you'll be buying bullocks next week!" Shirley clipped their wings so they couldn't fly away. "You obviously didn't know what you were buying," said George examining the birds, "you've got yourself four drakes - boys."

"How can you tell?" I asked, looking for the obvious signs. They all laughed and told me that drakes have a curly tuft on the end of their tail feathers. They were apparently Indian Runners, which I'd never heard of before, and would eat anything, especially boiled potato peelings.

Once back home we took George's advice and let them loose; I was rather doubtful but I realised that it was now or never, they couldn't stay in the box for ever. It was highly entertaining watching the ducks waddling about their new surroundings, but we knew if they decided to wander away we'd have no chance of finding them. We needn't have worried, the ducks seemed quite happy to stay in their new home, and then whilst we were watching them in the field I suddenly realised what they were missing.

"Water, we need to get them some water," I shouted. Dave nodded.

"I could hose them down gently," he suggested, "or we could give them the washing up bowl and buy a new one tomorrow."

"Don't be daft, they need something bigger than a washing up bowl - the boy's paddling pool." I said. "That will be ideal." Dave and the boys looked at me as if I was mad, but soon the paddling pool was inflated, filled with water and our four drakes were swimming round and round quacking merrily. We soon discovered ducks are not very good gardeners, they do not seem to know the difference between weeds and plants, and we had to watch them the whole day long. When night fell we knew the ducks would be in real danger of a fox getting them if we left them out, so we decided to put them in the outside toilet. However, they did not realise we were doing this for their own benefit and every time we tried to catch them they ran away. Half an hour later the outside loo was still duckless, so the boys came out to help and between us we finally coaxed them round the side of the cottage towards the duck house. Whilst doing all this we decided to name them, Ricky called his Donald (very original), John called his Loui, and I called mine Quacker, not only because he was the noisiest but also because I must have been quackers to buy them! Dave had not thought of a name for his but it was certainly giving us the run around. Donald, Loui and Quacker were all inside, but the last one was always too quick. Dave's patience was wearing thin by this time and pretty soon all sorts of names were being suggested; every time he made a dive for the duck it slipped through his hands. The boys and I were no help as we were curled up with laughter in the corner. It was now pitch dark and the boys went into the house to fetch a torch, and eventually Dave caught him and locked him in safely with the others.

"That one's name is Slippery." said Dave. So there we had it, Donald, Loui, Quacker and Slippery.

Next morning we were all up early to let the ducks out and feed them on scraps and the boiled potato peelings. My brother John, and Mac arrived ready for work as promised and the three men soon set off to start canvassing for new business.

I spent the day at home with the boys and made a large steak and kidney pie which was ready for their return later that evening. They had managed to secure twenty customers which was better than expected and showed there was genuine potential for the business. After dinner I sat writing out the new customers' names and addresses in the accounts books, not really believing that we were at last living and working in Devon.

John and Mac were full of fun and had us laughing each evening when they came home with more customers and tales of the people they had met during the day. They stayed until the Saturday and then returned to London, coming back to Devon the following Wednesday to canvass more customers. They did this for a few weeks, by which time we had the basis for a substantial business, without their help I doubt we would have managed it.

As time went by I realised we had not heard anything from our solicitor and the next month's mortgage would be due soon. We were banking on a settlement for our old house in London to help meet the payment and as things were there was no way we could possibly afford it. So next morning Dave went down to our local call box to do some chasing up and find out what the hold up was. When he came back I could tell from the expression on his face something was wrong. He explained there was a problem with our buyer's lease on her old property and it looked as if she wouldn't be able to sell. I couldn't believe it.

"Don't be stupid," I said, "we've signed the contracts, and she should have moved in this week. The solicitor said that everything was fine and nothing could go wrong." I couldn't take it in. It was like a brick hitting us between the eyes. All the planning we had done, all the hard work. It couldn't all go wrong, not now. "What do we do now?" I asked helplessly. Dave shrugged.

"It doesn't look good."

We got on to the bank and our building society right away but there was very little anyone could do. Obviously we now had to continue paying the mortgage on our old house in London as well as the mortgage on Bramble Cottage and the solicitor's fees. Our debts increased each month. The London house went back on the market and by a stroke of good fortune we had another buyer interested straight away due to the attractive price. We were working really hard and saving money wherever we could, but we were finding it impossible to make ends meet. Then disaster - more bad news. Our second buyer pulled out because he had just been made redundant. Things were going from bad to worse, it looked as if the house in London would have to be repossessed and we were facing serious arrears on our cottage. We couldn't afford to pay the two mortgages as well as the bills that were mounting up. Our whole life was falling apart, what had we done? Our Devon dream was becoming a nightmare.

We decided to put our London house up for sale with several estate agents and also to change our solicitors. We felt they hadn't done much for us except send us a large bill. By now we would be selling at a huge loss no matter what happened and it seemed likely we would be paying for it for ever. We were only a small business and the debt was way out of our depth. The stress started to affect our health, we were not sleeping and constantly worrying ourselves sick about the future. We started to miss the odd day off work because we felt so low it just didn't seem worth making the effort. However many customers we had and however much we earned it would never be enough to make any difference to our debts. Some days it was costing more in petrol to go to work than we were taking from selling our goods. It was a desperate struggle to find the will power to get up each day and go about our business. This went on for months, Dave would comfort me and tell me not to worry and at other times I would try to comfort him and say that as long as we were together everything would be alright. But deep down we were both frightened and feared we were finished.

Eventually we found another buyer for our London house. We had been living in Devon for nearly a year when the solicitor phoned to say that we were due to complete on the 17th January, but the problem was the building society proposed to repossess on the same date. He had spoken to the building society and they promised to stop the repossession as long as the house was sold and they had their money on the same day in question. On the 15th January I spoke to our solicitor. He said that everything was going well and that I should give him a ring first thing on the 17th. Two days later in a state of nervous anticipation I rang their number again. A female voice answered and explained she was now handling our affairs and all the paperwork was going through quite smoothly. However, there had been a development their end but she reassured me our paperwork was still proceeding.

"What's the problem your end then?" I pestered.

"Well I'm afraid your solicitor committed suicide last night," she replied somewhat reluctantly.

A stunned silence followed, I couldn't take all this in. It had been thirteen months since we left London, thirteen months of worry, difficulties and a great deal of stress. At last the waiting was over and things would now be easier for us, but to finish with this news was just overwhelming. If anybody was going to commit suicide I would have thought it would have been us, not the solicitor. That evening a great cloud still hung over us and all we could think of was that poor man.

5
More Livestock

Despite the financial worries our way of life in Devon was a vast improvement on London. John had settled in well at school and from the first day everyone so was so kind and welcoming, something that he never experienced in London. It was a lovely walk to John's school along the leafy country lanes instead of trying to cross the main roads in London, defying the traffic. On his first day they let him pull the rope to ring the big old fashioned school bell that hung on the wall. During the afternoons I walked along the lane with Ricky to meet John, saying hello to just about everyone, and on the way home Ricky would pick me a bunch of flowers, weeds really, from the roadside and John would chat non-stop about his day at school, about all the other children and what they had been doing. It was a delight to see his little face grinning with pleasure as he skipped and jogged home. It was moments like this which made me feel everything was going to work out fine.

We made another visit to the livestock market and this time Hazel came with us. Dave didn't look at all surprised when I started bidding for two cockerels, and Hazel just laughed.

"You'll have to move to a farm at this rate," she joked as we were trying to get the birds out of the cage. They looked massive. "Whatever you do," said Hazel, "keep hold of their wings and don't let go."

The first one was no problem, I just lifted him into the box, but as I lifted the second one it slipped out of my hand and started flapping his wings, took off and flew right over the auctioneer's head. I have never seen so many people duck so fast in my life! Hazel was laughing, Dave was embarrassed, and I was wishing I was somewhere else. Eventually a farmer caught hold of the bird by the leg and slipped him into the box. Everybody was still looking at us as we walked hurriedly out of the market.

Of course we stopped at George and Esther's to get some advice about our latest purchase, this time cockerel management.

"Just let them go," was his advice, but I wasn't so sure.

They seemed friendly but we watched them out of the corner of our eyes as though we were watching a new born baby. They strutted around as if telling the world that the 'guvnors' had arrived, inspecting every nook and cranny and looking for tit-bits to eat. It was later in the day I realised that the cockerels had not been 'cockering' or doing what cockerels do. We popped into George's before collecting John from school and queried it with him.

"What did you say?" I thought he'd not heard me but it turned out to be in sheer disbelief at what I had said. I repeated myself adding,

"I was wondering if it's possible to buy duff cockerels as I haven't heard my two cockering yet." Well, he just roared with laughter and told everyone in sight, and probably those not in sight, how silly I was, correcting me that it wasn't cockering but crowing. He was still laughing as we left to pick up John. I told him about our two new farmyard friends and what do you think we heard when we came back home? Our cockerels were crowing. It mattered little what it was called, it sounded great even if they were twelve hours too early. During the evenings it was a pleasure to sit out the back of the cottage and watch the ducks and the cockerels. Loui kept poking one of the cockerels with his beak, a real comical sight, he was the skinniest of the ducks but by far the sauciest. We were getting really attached to our new acquisitions and even Judy watched over them with ears cocked.

Another evening Dave walked in with a small box under his arm and a sheepish look on his face.

"I met a new customer today," he said. "she didn't have a deposit to put down on the goods she wanted but she did have a load of baby rabbits." He didn't have to say any more.

"Let me have a look," I cried, and there in the box was a beautiful baby rabbit, white with a grey streak down his back. So this was our next animal, we were getting to be quite a crowd.

Hoppity had to stay in the box for the night, I gave him a saucer of milk, some carrot and a piece of cold crisp toast, which rabbits are supposed to like for their teeth. The boys were delighted to have a rabbit of their own, and we set off early next morning to the wood merchants to buy some wood. It was only for a rabbit hutch we explained and the assistant immediately downed his tools and went off to rummage in a store around the back.

"I know just what you want," he said and ended up drawing all these diagrams with Dave watching over his shoulder. Finally we loaded all the wood into the van and drove home. For the rest of the day Dave worked on Hoppity's home and when it was finished it was superior to anything you would buy in a shop. It was more like a bungalow than a rabbit hutch; we put in the sawdust the wood merchant had given us and it looked so cosy that I could have moved in there myself. Hoppity seemed very pleased with his new home.

The following Saturday afternoon the school held their annual fete and we all walked across the fields in the hazy sunshine, clutching the cakes I'd made for the cake stall. It was a real family affair and the boys were allowed to run and play in the fields. I had never been able to let them out of my sight before.

Sunday afternoon Jan popped in and asked me if I would like to go with her to see the horses she looked after a mile or so away. We walked for ages through fields, over streams and through a wood where she told me deer grazed. Finally we reached the field where Bill and his mate Dopey came trotting over to see us. The setting was beautiful and Jan pointed out some wild orchids growing in the grass. On the other side of the field was an old barn where an elderly gentleman used to keep his horses. Jan explained he had lived locally for years with his horses but now lived in a residential home. It must have been wonderful for him to walk up here every morning to see them. Jan remembered walking up here as a child to ride Bill and see Dopey. Now she visited the old gent every week to tell him how his horses were. Just down the road were the remains of a large bonfire, Jan told me it was the site of the old gent's caravan. Just opposite was a much newer caravan with a goat and a dog outside. Apparently they were squatters, but turned out to be really nice people, perhaps history was repeating itself, or perhaps there was a court order already on its way to evict them.

6
School Holidays

Come summer we had really settled into our new way of life and it was suiting us perfectly, although we realised it would be a several years before we could claim to be locals. John and Ricky were so healthy and happy, enjoying everything that the countryside had to offer. The country air was doing them the world of good. They often went up to Hazel's for tea, her garden was an abundance of poppies and put mine to shame, but I think that was due to me planting the seeds very late.

We loved exploring the lanes around the village, looking at the cottages, all of them different and all full of character. One in particular was especially beautiful with an old thatched roof and an old crooked bench outside, piled with pots of geraniums. It had red and white climbing roses growing around the doors and a thriving cottage garden. Nicki, the play school teacher, her husband Tony and their two children lived there and one day we casually popped in to see them while passing. Inside was a dream, everything so homely and welcoming, a real Devon cottage home. Nicki said that everything was original and the cottage dated back to the sixteenth century.

On the way home we noticed a footpath leading off through the hedgerow and as we were in no hurry we decided to see where it led. We walked across some fields, through sheep grazing on the lush grass, up a hill and down a hill, and came across the remains of an old manor house. Apparently it had burnt down during the 1960s, and rumour has it that it had been full of antiques which had mysteriously vanished prior to the fire being discovered. The story goes on to relate that when the caretaker discovered the blaze he walked to the local pub, over three miles away, and before phoning the fire brigade ordered a pint and bought a packet of crisps. Needless to say the fire was well under way by the time the firemen arrived, and despite their considerable efforts they could not save the house. It was a sad sight now, you could still make out the shell of the house and the big old-fashioned doorways. The remains were covered with creeping bracken and rhodedendrons were growing everywhere. In its day it must have been a grand country manor house. We also saw some deer, they were beautiful, but they didn't appreciate our presence and quickly ran off to the protection of the thick woods. The trees stretched as far as the eye could see on land owned by the National Trust.

As the sun dipped it made everything appear bright and clean, with an orange tint reaching out across the sky. Dartmoor looked very close, its proud ancient hills dominating the skyline. They looked beautiful from this distance and yet at the same time almost foreboding, it made me shiver imagining being lost out there in winter in the fog or the snow.

John and Mac were still spending the occasional day helping us canvass new customers, the numbers were mounting though of course with the recession it was bound to be very hard going, even with the three men working together. One day the heavens opened and it was impossible to work in the torrential rain, so they had no choice but to take the day off. They weren't very pleased as they had driven nearly two hundred miles to go to work and wanted to get on with it. But there was no point in saturating the stock as well as themselves so an enforced day off had to be taken. By mid-afternoon the rain had eased and we had the chance to take a quick walk around the field. Water was dripping and running everywhere and although the ducks were pleased to see us, no doubt wondering why we hadn't been out in the rain like them, the cockerels had not liked the rain one bit and we found them sheltering in the hedges looking very bedraggled and sorry for themselves.

That evening we arranged a baby-sitter and took John and Mac to our local pub a mile away. Good food and a few drinks soon lifted everyone's spirits and by the time we walked back around midnight the rain had stopped and everything smelt so wonderfully fresh. The moon was shining so bright we didn't even need a torch and somewhere in the half dark we could hear owls hooting. Something flew across my face and made me jump nearly out of my skin. It was a bat and we could make out several more darting to and fro. I had never seen one before let alone have one so close to me.

The following week held more surprises. After a trip to Holsworthy we popped in to see George and Esther, we hadn't seen them for a few days as they'd been very busy with the hay-making, although every time they passed our house they would sound the car horn to let us know that they were still about. Shirley was there and asked me if I would like to feed her horse some carrots, so we both went out into the pouring rain and for several minutes stood in the middle of a muddy field feeding carrots to a horse who was probably thinking what daft creatures humans are, for whilst he was protected from the elements by a large waterproof known as a New Zealand rug, I stood there in an anorak and within minutes was soaked to those items of clothing next to the skin. Shirley mentioned she had some kittens and took me over to see them. Three of them still needed homes, and when we went back into the farmhouse for a hot cup of tea and a drying out I was clutching two black kittens.

"Look what I've got Dave."

"Oh, they're nice," he said guardedly.

"What shall we call them?" I asked innocently.

"We can't have cats we've got a dog."

"Judy will be fine," I replied.

"No she won't, she hates cats."

"That's because she doesn't have any living with her, trust me, she'll be fine. In any case they will kill the rats."

"But we haven't got rats."

"No, but we might get some if we don't have a cat." Dave looked at George.

"Help," he said, "how can you argue with reasoning like that?"

George just laughed and remarked,

"I think you've lost that one Dave."

So there we were: four ducks, two cockerels, one rabbit and now two kittens. It's living spontaneously that adds spice to life and after all it was this attitude that got us out of London in the first place and into this beautiful part of the world.

The boys were delighted when they saw the kittens and for some reason promptly named them Sausage and Chips. Judy was fine and she certainly proved my point when one of the kittens came in soaking wet and totally bedraggled. She went up to her gently nudging her with her nose and proceeded to lick her dry like a mother cat.

Apart from our financial problems life was good and our home was perfect, but the reality was we really needed to increase our income and this was becoming our main concern. Work was a lot less stressful than it had been in London, but the shortage of money and the debts mounting up were causing us problems. When Dave went off to work on a Monday morning I couldn't help but feel guilty that while he was out there trying to do the business in all weathers, I was left to enjoy our cottage. I wanted to be at home but I wanted to help Dave as well. I felt useless, but I couldn't go far as we didn't have a second vehicle.

Whilst on one of the toddlers' days out with some of the other local mums, and visiting a local farm where the children helped feed the lambs and stroke the animals, one of the mums mentioned her sister was on the look-out for a pet rabbit that she wanted in exchange for a guinea pig. I told her about Hoppity and said that Dave could probably manage to get her one and in return I could have the guinea pig. She was delighted with this arrangement and very soon Dave obtained the rabbit and the boys got their guinea pig. We had also made friends with two big shire horses, stopping to say hello to them each time we passed their field. The two horses, Duke and Diane put their heads over the gate and nuzzled the boys knowing they'd always got some polo mints for them. As we walked on a bit further, Sandy, a neighbour's dog would come up and wag his tail and say hello. All these little things made life so different to London. All the animals were characters, even one of our cockerels had become cheeky enough to jump up on to the kitchen window sill and put his head through the open window to see what scraps he could pinch.

Another memory that will stay with us for ever was Shirley taking us to see a new-born foal in the stable. It was a lovely sight to see the little filly laying beside her mum in the straw. Her mum had been quite a successful steeplechaser. The foal was a bay (light brown) and Shirley informed me that there is an old saying that a bay horse with four white socks will not be a success, and many people will not buy one for this reason. Looking at this little beauty just a few hours old the colouring was impossible to make out but if we'd had the money I'd have taken the risk.

It was a glass of homemade lemonade at Pat's house one scorching July afternoon that began our enjoyment of a new hobby. The lemonade was delicious and I asked Pat how she had made it. Elder flowers, lemon and sugar were the main ingredients, and she had got the recipe from a book intriguingly titled 'Fruity Passions'. I laughed to myself thinking about telling Dave I was going to buy a book called 'Fruity Passions', then informing him it was all about making wine and lemonade - what a let down! Anyway I found the book in the bookshop, and straight away had a go at making it myself. Not only did it taste good, but it was cheap and it was also great fun picking the elder flowers from the elder tree in the field. We hadn't even known that was what it was. The book also contained a number of wine recipes, hence the birth of our new hobby. On the way home after picking the boys up from school, we picked honeysuckle from the hedgerows. Norman the baker was due to call that evening so I planned to buy the rest of the ingredients from him. This I did and that night, with the boys tucked up in bed and Dave relaxing in his chair, I set to work. Later, surrounded by demi-johns and waiting for the sugar water to boil, Dave and I agreed that we could quite easily get used to this cheap entertainment.

July remained dry except for just the occasional wet day. One such day was a Sunday and the boys were a bit fed up so we took them and Jay, Pat's son, out for a drive. We couldn't see much as the rain made the countryside look so misty, and upon our return to Pat's farmhouse she said she had put in extra potatoes and we were to stay for Sunday roast. The dinner smelt delicious, it was roast pork (one of their own pigs) and was helped down with last year's honeysuckle wine.

In the evening we all put on our wellies and helped out with the chores. We helped feed the pigs and cows and then all trooped off to the fields to bring in a cow which was supposed to be acting as a foster mother to an orphaned calf, as well as looking after her own three day old offspring. Unfortunately she didn't want this strange calf and to make absolutely certain she wasn't letting it suckle from her , rejected her own calf as well. Once we had caught her we led her and the two calves into the barn and tethered her up so that she couldn't turn her head properly to see which one was hers, but she still kicked them both out of the way. Pat's husband Terry, said that he would have to leave her for a while in the barn and hope she would calm down and eventually let them both suck from her.

On returning to the farmhouse the smell of cooking still lingered in the kitchen but it was time for us to go home and upon leaving promised to return the hospitality very soon. Mulling things over on the way back to Bramble Cottage I realised how fortunate we were to be living in such an idyllic way and not even the thought of all our debts and the ever present worry of living on the edge, finance wise, could sadden me.

Two weeks later we decided to drive out to Bude, about twenty miles away. We managed to find a secluded beach and as the tide was out we were able to walk over the rocks and explore the pools. We found little jelly fish, crabs and lots of small fish, as well as all sorts of debris lying along the tide line. The salt air was really invigorating and as the tide came in the waves increased and soon they were crashing into the bottom of the cliffs. In the space of a few hours the peacefulness we found when arriving had changed and the mood had become somewhat dramatic, wild, and in a way almost foreboding. I suppose if you live beside the seaside you get used to these mood changes but to ex-townies like us it made us feel rather uneasy.

A few days later it was the school sports day. This was John's first sports day and Dave really wanted to attend but he just couldn't spare the time from work. However, Pat came to meet me and as we were a bit late we cut across the fields at the back of our cottage. We had a great afternoon. All the mums had turned out to cheer the children on. In the mother's race I came second, but it was judged to have been a false start and in the re-run I came second last. Everyone got involved and we all thoroughly enjoyed the afternoon. On the way home we cut across the fields as before and I, dressed in my white blouse and white skirt specially for the occasion, slipped and fell head long into several cow pats. I looked and smelt lovely but with the children and Pat laughing their socks off, managed to see the funny side of it.

The school summer holidays were nearly upon us and just before the term closed the school held a parent's evening. John's teacher told us how well he had settled in and how popular he was with the other children. We were very pleased to hear this but I knew by the way he skipped out of school with the other children, always smiling and full of his news that he was perfectly happy. I looked forward to having him home for six weeks, we might not have much money but we were free to laugh and play and go for long walks, and the boys had as much space to play outside as they could ever want.

We hadn't seen Sausage our cat for a while and we were getting worried about her. We had driven all around the lanes looking for her and asked everybody if they had seen her, but there was no sign. We even put up notices on the gate posts but eventually we had to accept something had happened to her, and we would not see her again.

A village fete was being held in a large garden a mile or so up the road, they were serving cream teas, along with other refreshments and amongst the many attractions were clay pigeon shooting and a thatching demonstration. After trying our hand at several of the activities on offer we got home rather late, and when I went to lock up the ducks that evening something came running towards me which I thought at first may have been Sausage but soon realised it was a fox, after my ducks. Luckily my presence scared him away.

During the school holidays we often took advantage of the Wednesday bus into town with Hazel and her children. We'd walk to the top of her lane to catch it and pile on with our swimming things as we were headed for the swimming pool. The town pool was very clean. There were no water slides or any of the other attractions associated with modern swimming pools, just a plain pool, but it was much cheaper than I expected. After swimming we'd have a coffee in a very old and quaint coffee house but we always had to keep an eye on the time as the bus only passes our way once a week!

On one occasion on arriving back home I took the five children and Judy out for a walk. We found a nest of mice and also observed a frog hopping down the road. The children were all feeling pretty excited as we struggled up one of the steepest hills I'd ever climbed. Ricky was in his pushchair as he was tired out after all the swimming and it required considerable effort pushing him up-hill. Judy did her bit pulling on the lead and the four children pushed me from behind, what a sight we must have been. I was wondering if we would ever make it to the top, puffing wildly and trying to keep a smile on my face. Well make it we did and the descent was probably steeper than the ascent, and from having Judy and the children pulling and pushing me up hill, I was now hanging on to them to avoid tumbling over and finishing in a heap at the bottom. Eventually we made it safely down the other side and walked a few yards to the stream which runs through the valley. It didn't take long for the children to get their boots and socks off to go paddling, I thought they would have had enough swimming for one day. I was in the process of making myself nice and comfortable on the ground and resting before tackling that hill again, when out of the blue, just over my shoulder came a loud MOO! I looked round to come face to face with the biggest Friesian cow I have ever seen, not that I had ever been this close to one of them before except in the milking shed back on George's farm. The blood drained from my face and trying not to use any swear words whilst keeping my head at the same time was no easy task. I asked Hazel's children what their mother would do in similar circumstances, they just carried on playing and said not to take any notice. That was a lot easier said than done. The cow took another step closer and nuzzled the carrier bag I had beside me.

"Come on, we're off." I shouted, and I was off up the hill pushing the empty pushchair with one hand and dragging poor Ricky along with the other. I left the children to fend for themselves. I could hear them running along behind me, hopefully with their boots and socks in their hands, but I couldn't bear to turn round to see if they were alright, for as long as my two legs had life in them I was getting up the hill to safety. After having such a struggle to climb the hill earlier it was quite remarkable to find the energy a second time so readily available. Judy was running about in circles barking madly, thinking it was all a great game and the children were all laughing at me, trying to persuade me that it was perfectly safe to go down to the stream again. I was having no more of that game. We made our way home and before returning to Hazel's I made myself a nice cup of tea and took a well earned rest. The children took great delight in telling her all about my predicament with the cow and needless to say Hazel found it all very amusing. Anyway that is one afternoon in the countryside that I won't forget in a hurry!

Having a pony of my own had always been one of my childhood dreams, I have always loved horses and although very uncertain around cows have no fears of being in close proximity to horses. So I was delighted to be asked by Jan one day if I would like to groom Bill, the horse that used to graze on our land before we purchased it. She was entering him in the local horse show later that day and was really pushed for time. I jumped at the chance, pulled on my old wellies and hurried up to Bill's field. He whinnied 'hello' to me as I got out the grooming kit, and full of enthusiasm I began my task. By the time Jan arrived I was sitting having a cup of coffee with Hazel, with Bill and the other show ponies all groomed and looking really smart. Jan asked me if I would like to enter Dopey, her other pony, in the best kept veteran class. I jumped at the chance. We soon set off down the lane with our ponies, they knew something was up as we clipped-clopped along towards the show ground, half a mile away. Silly as it might sound I was becoming very nervous and the wait for our class at the show seemed endless. Dopey became quite restless and despite me walking him around on the lead-rein showed a lot of energy for a veteran. The thought crossed my mind that perhaps nobody had actually told him he was a veteran. Finally our class was called,

"Wish us luck," I called to Dave and the boys who had come along to watch us. Nervously I led Dopey around the show ring. I'm not sure whether I was supporting him, or he was supporting me, but we seemed to get on very well together, or so I thought. When called we had to walk up to the judge and parade around on our own before lining up again with the others. We came sixth and I proudly collected our rosette before returning home on cloud nine. I had always dreamed of competing in a horse show and at last my dream had come true, even if it wasn't with my own horse!

Just before the close of the school holidays we all went again to the livestock market taking Hazel's three children with us as well. This time there were many more visitors and holiday-makers and the market was crowded. The animals were fetching far higher prices and I wondered if all the people bidding for the animals would actually look after them once the novelty wore off. There was a completely different atmosphere in the market but I did manage to buy six bantams to go with the cockerels, and to save them going to bad homes, and fifteen ducks, seven of which were tiny ducklings. Dave was standing outside and he nearly had a fit when I told him. I thought by now he would have got used to my impulse buying of furry and feathered varieties.

"How many?" he shrieked. "I thought you might get some chickens but not more ducks."

"I felt sorry for them." It was the only excuse I could come up with.

"Oh Sonya," he said looking at me doubtfully, "you and your animals."

"I know," I said with a smile, "but you wouldn't have me any other way would you?" He gave a faint smile, much to my relief. However, it was a scorching hot day and the poor things were panting before we even got them out of their cages, and by the time we got home four of the ducklings had died, the heat had been too much for them. We lightly hosed the others down and soon they were happily splashing about in the paddling pool. Now we had problems with all these additional feathered friends. The outside toilet, which doubled as the duck house, could not accommodate them all, so Dave and I set to work with pencil and ruler and after much discussion, much drawing and much erasing, managed to produce the plans for a grand duck house. Come the weekend we took our plans to the woodyard and purchased the necessary requirements. As soon as we got home we unloaded all the wood and Dave set to work. He really worked hard on it, I could hear sawing, hammering, whistling, humming and every so often a shout for assistance, and of course the occasional (occasional?) swear word. Twenty four hours later the duck house was complete. It even had a section for the hens with a long broom handle fixed across where they could roost at night, and nesting boxes where they would hopefully lay their eggs. Dave was very proud of it and rightly so. We put straw inside and a large bowl of water, and as we escorted the ducks into their new house they all quacked with delight. The chickens however had decided to have none of it and had taken refuge in the hedges. Trying to retrieve them was really comical, Dave was chasing them on one side of the hedge while I was chasing them on the other. We soon learned to leave them there and let them come back of their own accord.

We told George and Esther about our duck house and later in the week they came over to view it. They had a good laugh at it as their birds all run free range twenty-four hours a day. George remarked that we would be putting in tables and chairs for them next.

All too soon the school holidays came to a close. Money may have been tight and special treats were few but we'd had the peace and beauty of the countryside and each other. As I looked out of our back window and across the fields towards the school, I could hear all the children playing happily together. After school John had been invited home to play with his friend Jay where he helped with the cows and watched Jay's dad baling with the tractor and the binding machine. He was full of it when he came home and couldn't stop talking about the farm. While John was with Jay I took Ricky for a walk as the evening was so lovely. We took an old margarine tub out with us to see if we could find any blackberries. Ricky hadn't started school yet and we often went for little walks together, watching and listening to all the birds and insects. One day we sat quietly together in a corner of a field watching the sheep grazing. There was nothing to be heard apart from them munching the grass. Two butterflies chasing each other fluttered past our noses, and I couldn't help thinking the closest I had ever got to this kind of peacefulness before was sitting on Mitcham Common watching the double decker buses going by.

7
A Busy Life

Autumn was approaching and as we walked home from school each day we watched the leaves beginning to change colour, some were already falling. After making a fuss of the shire horses in the field, we started to collect some of the fallen leaves, horse chestnut, elder and hawthorn, to make leaf rubbings and autumn pictures. The boys love doing things like this whilst sitting beside our log fire. One such evening around this time we were in the barn feeding the rabbit when we heard the lid of the old-fashioned apple jar lying nearby being banged. Thinking that Judy must have knocked it with her tail we thought no more about it, but a few seconds later it banged again. Judy was standing there with her head cocked to one side, looking intently towards the jar. We stood perfectly still for a moment and then I ventured towards the apple jar saying,

"You silly old dog, there's nothing in there." I lifted the lid to satisfy her curiosity, and WOOSH, out of the jar sprang one of the chickens, flapping wildly and clucking as it ran around. The boys had run out of the barn and while my heart returned to its proper place I noticed Judy had also disappeared and even the rabbit had run into his corner, ears flat in fright. I called Judy back and calmed her down, then fed the rabbit and eventually shooed the chicken outside, but how on earth it got inside the jar with the lid on is a mystery.

We hadn't been collecting many eggs in our duck come hen house and a local farmer told me not to let the chickens out before mid-day as they would lay elsewhere. A few days later the farmer was cutting the hedges in the field next to ours and as the bushes were gradually getting lower, Ricky could see the driver and stood waving at him. The farmer noticed him and drove over to trim our hedge and it was when the hedges had been cut down that we found out just where the chickens had been laying their eggs. All told we collected over two dozen from beneath the bushes.

We came home from a shopping trip one morning to find Sam, Jan's husband excavating a large hole at the end of our field with his mechanical digger. He had promised us he would make a large duck pond for us after laughing at the ducks in the children's paddling pool. We had to save up for a couple of weeks or so before we could afford a large black plastic sheet pond liner which we pegged out and weighted down with rocks all around the edges. It took nearly all day to fill up from the hose pipe. The ducks followed us everywhere, we had a duck and a drake who were virtually inseparable, Missus being the dominant one was first into the new pond, followed by Mister. They submerged their heads and splashed about, obviously delighted with their new pond and it seemed well worth the financial struggle to pay Sam just to see their delight.

September 28th saw John's sixth birthday and knowing how much he loved playing with toy farms we popped into Holsworthy to buy a large wooden farmyard that he'd had his eye on for several months. To see his face while he was setting it all up was a picture. Naturally we had a birthday party for him in the afternoon and almost all the children from the village gathered in Bramble Cottage for the party. They had a great time playing all the usual games and filled the cottage with laughter. Money was still very tight and we didn't have much to offer but the sight of all those happy little faces was heart-warming.

Some early mornings before Dave went to work, we would all stroll down the lanes looking at the autumn colours and the green fields still covered with the early morning dew and occasional light frosts. It was so quiet and peaceful and we would think to ourselves how lucky we were to be living like this. One morning we returned to find a cow right outside our front gate and Dave had to shoo her back into the field. He blocked up the gap in the hedge as best he could to prevent the cow getting out again and I told Stan, the farmer, about it when he came down later to tend the cows. He thanked me and was in the field for ages repairing the hedge. Sadly, a few days later, we noticed a dead cow in the field and we all watched from the window as they loaded the carcass into a lorry. All the other cows stood around and watched as though paying their last respects. Stan remarked that as a farmer he had quickly learned that where ever you have livestock you will always get dead stock.

Another cow passed our gate one morning but this time it was one of George's. She had also managed to get out of her field and come up the road to see all her mates, I phoned George.

"Put the kettle on and I'll be right on up." When he saw the cow in the field he said that he might as well leave her there as she seemed quite happy. "The bugger will only get out again," he said and came in for his tea.

George mentioned they had some kittens. As we hadn't seen Sausage for some time I thought I would go and have a look at them and maybe give one a good home. I fell in love with a tiny ginger and white one, the prettiest little thing I'd ever seen, so home it came and was promptly named Top Cat. She turned out to be a real tinker, exceptionally nosey and able to get in anywhere, the wardrobe, the tumble dryer, you name it. She would play for hours in the field chasing the feathers blowing around in the wind.

Early one morning I was awoken by the sound of a cry below our bedroom window. It was still dark so there was no point looking out but I was sufficiently awake to know that it was a fox. Quickly I turned to Dave and said,

"There's a fox after me ducks," but the only response was a loud snore. I jumped out of bed and whilst shaking Dave with one hand and grabbing my dressing gown with the other John came in half asleep.

"What's up mum?" he asked.

"There's a bloomin' fox after me ducks and your father won't wake up!" John climbed on to the bed and started to shake Dave. He eventually woke up and when the emergency of the situation sunk in staggered to his feet and started to reach for his dressing gown.

"No time for that," I shouted and pushed him out of the bedroom. He led the way downstairs with me behind, John following and Judy bringing up the rear. She, the faithful hound, had come out from underneath the bed and tagged on to the end of the convoy. Armed with torches we rushed over to the duck house only to find them all fast asleep and on being disturbed no doubt thinking that our alarm clock had gone off early. Naturally the fox had long gone, what with all the commotion we were making he was probably in Cornwall. Dave locked the duck house door again and stood there shaking his head in disbelief. The only clothing he was wearing was his underpants, he was not amused but I saw the funny side of it all and burst in to uncontrollable laughter. As I rocked backwards and forwards, holding my sides, John joined in and even Judy appeared to be grinning until she thought better of it and returned to the safety of the bedroom again. Back indoors I put on the kettle and asked Dave if he would like a cup of tea, I think he muttered something rude under his breath! Next time Mr Fox comes visiting I shall go out and look for him on my own.

There was another horse show during October and Jan asked me if I would like to help. Naturally I was delighted to do so and as we walked across the fields to collect Bill, once again a feeling of excitement crept over me. Bill stopped grazing and slowly walked over to greet us. We each took it in turns to brush his coat and oil his hooves while he stood patiently tied to the gate. When he was ready I led him to the show field while Jan took the children along in the car. As we walked along I talked to him all the time and he seemed to nod in appreciation, perhaps he understood my every word. I kept telling him what a smart lad he was but he knew that already. Last minute preparations were hastily conducted and we watched as Jan led Bill into the show ring. They looked really smart and Bill was behaving perfectly, but then so did all the rest and I began to appreciate how difficult a job the judge had. Bill came third which we were all very pleased with and I proudly walked him home displaying another rosette.

The school held a Hallowe'en party and the children were in their element dressed up in black hats and cloaks made out of what I was told were old Second World War black-out curtains. There were cakes and sandwiches cut out in the shape of bats, green cakes with jelly snakes on the top and best of all, a giant pumpkin with a face carved out of it. With the candle lit inside, it looked very spooky. I had never seen it done before.

As a rule Judy got on well with the hens, she didn't seem to bother about them at all, but one day, as I was standing at the kitchen sink peeling potatoes, I heard such a commotion that I rushed outside to see what was happening. I found one of our hens huddled in a corner frightened to death. It looked as if it had had its rear end bitten off and was bleeding badly with some of its intestines hanging out. I really scolded Judy and she knew she had done something wrong as she immediately cowered, I couldn't understand what had come over her, it was totally out of character, but now my main concern was the hen. I didn't know what to do for her although I must admit if I'd been able to do it I would have rung her neck. I made her as comfortable as possible on a bale of straw and then phoned George. He was out on the farm somewhere but Esther told me to bring the hen down to the farm. The boys were home so we all trudged down the road in the rain with me clutching the hen wrapped in an old towel. We met George in the farmyard,

"Hello Sonya, what you be about then?" I showed him the hen and explained what had happened, he carefully looked her over.

"You can't kill a chicken just for that." he said finally.

"But George, she's in pain and been bitten nearly in half and all her insides are hanging out." Well, George took one look at me and said in his usual bellowing voice,

"If Esther wrung my neck every time I had a bit hanging out I'd be in terrible trouble." We both laughed and I was still laughing to myself on the way home, once again clutching the chicken. It did take some weeks to heal but as always George was proved right and soon she was as good as new. Every now and then George would pop in to see how she was getting on and every time he would say,

"She'll be fine, it's healing that bit better." Sure enough a few weeks later she started laying eggs again.

November brought bitter cold evenings but often we had to work late into the night completing the day's returns and doing the books. One evening I suggested we siphon off some of the wine for Christmas.

"Why don't we have a go tonight?" Dave suggested. So we looked out my Fruity Passions wine book to read how to go about it. Dave started while I finished off a few jobs and put the animals to bed. Whilst I was tidying up the living room I heard slurred curses coming from the kitchen. Dave isn't a big drinker and has been known to act the fool now and then, so I didn't take any notice. Five minutes later he popped his head round the door to tell me that I would have to do the rest as it was quite strong stuff. He swayed and his eyes appeared glazed and he promptly sat down in the armchair and fell asleep. It must be good stuff I thought, and went about siphoning off another couple of gallons. I concluded it wasn't really ready yet but hopefully by Christmas we should have a bottle or two. After getting Dave to bed I slept very soundly on the after effects myself.

We'd agreed we couldn't really afford to take the boys to a firework display that year and besides they were quite young and might be frightened. However, a note came from the school saying that the local pub was holding a small display for the village children.

"Can we go?" they asked. So on the night we had a big pot of stew and dumplings, put on double layers of jumpers and set off with our torches to the pub about a mile away. Most of the children were there, obviously all very excited. The fireworks popped, banged and whooshed and we all oohed and aahed and occasionally shrieked. Afterwards the majority of the parents gathered in the pub for a drink while all the children played together outside. Unfortunately Dave had to hear about it all second-hand as he had not been able to get home in time to come with us.

We discovered one of the drawbacks of living in the countryside when Dave came home from work one day complaining of a bad back. He could hardly move and we had no alternative than to call out the doctor even though it was very late. Dr. Wardle gave Dave some painkillers and waited a while to ensure they had the required effect. Half an hour later he was still in great pain and she proposed admitting him to Barnstaple hospital. I hated the thought of him being so far away and begged her to let him stay at home. Although it was nearly midnight, she said she would call back later in the night to see how he was doing. When she returned he was obviously no better and she immediately called the ambulance. It arrived within twenty minutes and within the hour Dave was in hospital. Living where we do I could hardly pop next door and ask a neighbour to look after the children whilst I accompanied him to the hospital. A tear ran down my cheek as I waved goodbye. First thing next morning I phoned to see how he was. The nurse who answered asked me to hold a moment.

"Just like London," I thought aloud, "they will keep me hanging on for ages and then pass me on to someone else." But I was in for a surprise, she soon came back on the line again and apologised for keeping me waiting and informed me Dave was able to speak to me himself. I imagined they had a mobile phone but he said they had wheeled his bed to the desk out in the corridor where the main phone was.

Word soon got around the village that Dave was in hospital. Neighbours rang continually inquiring as to his well being and there were so many kind offers of help. The hospital diagnosed the problem as being a trapped nerve and after twenty four hours of traction he was released the next day and told to have a week's bed rest. It was so good to have him home again, being apart doesn't suit us at all. I'm thankful he's not a long distance lorry driver.

By the time Dave was able to resume work Christmas was only five weeks away and we had bills that needed settling. To be honest the last thing we wanted was the expense of Christmas, but we had noticed the boys were far more content and not asking for the expensive toys advertised on television. They knew we had to watch the pennies and anyway were happier playing outside and enjoying many of the things in life that come free. We had a lot of fun together and made up games instead of buying them, and probably enjoyed them all the more.

We did allow them one special treat when Dave returned to work. We took them to the Holsworthy carnival procession. Although it was a bitterly cold night thousands of spectators lined the streets clapping and cheering the brilliantly decorated floats as they slowly filed past. The atmosphere was tremendous and we all thoroughly enjoyed it. To round off a perfect evening I treated the family to a fish and chip supper, although we had to queue for nearly an hour because the shop was so busy.

With winter rapidly approaching we made plans to stock up on supplies, not only for ourselves but also for the animals. Living here between Dartmoor and Exmoor we had been told it's not uncommon to be cut off from the usual services for several days at a time. I had already filled the freezer with beef and lamb when we were offered a pig. We were rather surprised to find it arrive more or less whole, less its insides. We turned the carcass this way and that trying to work out how best to cut it up but in the end admitted defeat and took it along to some friends for professional advice. They were soon cutting it up into various joints and packs and not a bit was wasted, we would never have managed it ourselves.

The next day we had a huge pile of logs delivered, they arrived so early I was pushing wheel barrowfuls around before I had barely opened my eyes. After that came a truck load of straw and hay bales for the animals which we piled high in the barn. The hens loved laying their eggs in the straw although through the winter they would lay very few. I also stocked up on corn and animal feeds so that the hens and the rest of the livestock would have plenty to eat. Finally I felt we were prepared for the winter and whatever it might bring.

49

Taking advantage of a free offer of a trip to town I picked out a lovely bushy Christmas tree and put a deposit on it. Our old artificial one would look all wrong in the cottage and anyway it had the look of an overgrown toilet brush as most of the bristles had fallen out. The new tree had a root ball and so hopefully we could plant it out and keep it for years to come. On the Saturday Dave collected it and when getting home we potted it and stood it in the barn ready to bring in and decorate nearer Christmas.

The next event in the calendar was the school Christmas play. On the evening of the big occasion a sharp frost had come down very early. Wrapping up well we all walked down to the school crunching the frost under our feet. It was a very clear night and bitterly cold but as soon as we arrived the cold chill melted away. The school hall was adorned with decorations and part of it was occupied with the stage and upright piano, with the audience packed in tightly in the remaining space. Eventually we were all seated, the lights dimmed and the headmaster appeared on stage to announce the proceedings. He light-heartedly informed us mistakes were bound to happen and we were just to enjoy them and laugh. Needless to say mistakes did occur but as instructed we all enjoyed them and laughed along with the children. Christmas carols and laughter filled the air, and we applauded all the various scenes. Afterwards tea and mince pies were served by the teachers and children, and if this was an example of the warmth and kindness of the local people we were certainly going to have fun this Christmas.

Pat and I agreed that it would be great fun to all have Christmas dinner together, they would come over to us after they had finished milking and the rest of the chores. Pat would supply a home reared turkey and we would supply the home-made wine. Boxing day we would spend with them and take the left-overs with us. This arrangement seemed a good idea and we were looking forward to it.

The school broke up for the Christmas break on December 22nd and with just one more day before Christmas Eve we started preparations in earnest, including finding sprigs of holly to put up and decorating the tree which now stood in the alcove by the fire. All last year's home-made decorations came out and although there were hundreds of them the boys still managed to argue over who should put the biggest ones up, and not quite all the chocolate decorations made it to the tree. The boys helped me blow up the balloons and hang up the Christmas cards. Finally I had a little time to myself to enjoy a cup of tea while the boys wrapped up Dave's present. The mince pies, sausage rolls and flans were cooling, the peppermint creams were setting and I still had a few minutes before I had to start preparing the turkey.

On Christmas Eve Dave came home early with more bags of shopping and a mysterious parcel which quickly disappeared upstairs. After tea I dressed up as Father Christmas and with my three 'elves' started delivering Christmas presents to all our friends. Everywhere we were made very welcome and our final call was on George and Esther. They were busy on the farm getting bales of hay out for the cattle. The kettle was on the Aga as usual and the cream was thickening on the top of the stove. Across the yard through the blackness of the night we could see the lights on in the barns where the cows were being milked. The boys went off to help with the milking while we stayed in the kitchen and opened a bottle of sherry and waited for George and Esther to finish their chores. By the time we returned to Bramble cottage we could hear the church bells ringing in the distance. Dave read the boys a goodnight Christmas story while I wrapped up a few remaining presents and when he came down we turned out all the lights and sat with just the Christmas tree lights twinkling in the darkness while we enjoyed a night cap. We tip-toed upstairs to grab a few hours sleep before Santa's sleigh arrived early next morning. It wasn't long before we heard the shouts of joy and delight from the boys when they discovered that Santa had been!

Dave had to find his Christmas present from John and Ricky by following a series of clues and they had him running around the house at six o'clock Christmas morning. One clue even took him out to the barn and he did look funny running about in his dressing gown in the darkness. Mind you he was sight happier than the last time we had him running about outside in just his underwear. The rest of the day was wonderful with several neighbours dropping in to wish us a happy Christmas and of course Pat, Terry and Neville arriving for Christmas dinner. They stayed much later than intended and before leaving echoed our feelings about the day. As the log fire died down and the embers slowly dimmed and lost their heat, it was time for bed.

We celebrated the New Year very quietly, just Dave, myself and the boys. Come midnight we raised our glasses and toasted the future. Although very happy with our new life in Devon, the new year had to see an improvement in our financial position and we were determined it would do.

One morning I went into the barn and noticed two green eyes staring at me. It was a black cat, and when I spoke to him he darted off. Next day he was back again so this time I left a saucer of milk out for him and some cat food, I thought he looked like a 'Blackie' but he took no notice when I called him, although he eagerly lapped up the milk. He soon became rather too friendly and I wished I hadn't put food down for him as it seemed we had a new member of the family. We found out he belonged to the landlord of our local pub and had been greatly missed. His name was Michael Angelo; no wonder he didn't answer to the name of Blackie. One morning the following week I heard a noise outside the back door and when I opened it to investigate in ran Michael Angelo. He looked me straight in the eyes and miaowed as if to say 'Can I stay - it's hard work, all this walking to and fro.' I phoned the landlord again and he suggested we keep him, I don't think either of us had much say in the matter. I'm not sure if we adopted him or he adopted us.

Mister and Missus, our ducks, were driving us quackers, they had decided to explore the immediate countryside and kept waddling off into the distance. Missus was the decision maker while Mister, who idolised her, kept one step behind at all times. One morning I discovered they were missing, I was very worried a fox might have had them. We left the barn door open in case they should return, but in my heart I felt we would never see them again. However, that evening I went out to shut the barn door and to our great relief they were waddling up the lane chatting away to each other obviously delighted with their day out. They headed straight back into the barn completely unaware and unconcerned as to the worry they had caused us. This was just the beginning of their great adventures, we never knew where they were and different people would return the ducks from all over the place, Missus used to waddle along constantly nagging Mister who would be obediently following and returning her quacks as if saying 'yes dear, yes dear,' while looking absolutely shattered after the mileage they had obviously covered. Soon the local motorists learned to slow down when passing our cottage in case Mister and Missus were having a wander. I tried every known thing to make them stay at home but nothing worked. Another morning a neighbour phoned to say she and her husband had been woken by strange noises outside their bedroom window and had discovered Mister and Missus sitting on the lawn chatting to each other without a care in the world. She sent them home straight away. They also found another neighbour's ornamental pond greatly to their liking and would swim up and down for hours. I spent a good hour in the pouring rain in a neighbour's farmyard trying to direct Missus back to her proper home, I knew Mister would follow. When I got them home we locked them in the duck house for a week, but as soon as I let them out again they promptly went walkabout, and that

52

evening a whole string of ducks waddled up the lane towards me with guess who as their ringleader? Missus, followed as ever by the faithful Mister, had taken all our ducks for a day out. This was the last straw, we had to put Missus in a long run and let Mister roam about with the others. Though they caused a great deal of trouble I will always remember the antics of that duo with great affection. Missus finally died of old age, and Mister died just a few days later, probably of a broken heart. Without Missus he just sulked in the corner, not eating, not quacking, not taking any interest. But I know no two ducks ever had a better life and I like to think of them still together, Mister and Missus.

One evening when the baker called he asked how long we'd had the sheep.

"What sheep?" we asked.

"The sheep in your back garden."

"We haven't got any sheep in the back garden."

"Yes you have, there's about fifty of them out there."

We all looked and saw he was right. We phoned the farmer and together we managed to drive them back to their own field. In the morning there were hundreds of hoof prints and bits of fleece sticking on the fences and hedges.

We decided to take the boys to the local drama group's pantomime, 'Dick Whittington.' We were not expecting too much but once again how wrong we all were. We should have known better, the band was excellent, the costumes were marvellous and the actors were really good. The audience were thoroughly entertained and showed their appreciation by asking for several curtain calls at the close of the show. We recognised a few of the cast as being local farm workers and shop assistants.

We were invited to another little show being held in the church hall and performed by several of our neighbours, with all proceeds going to church improvements. Not being churchgoers we were pleased to be invited and it showed us yet another side of rural life we had never experienced before.

The winter was mainly quite a mild one with the daffodils in bloom by mid February, closely followed by the primroses and a few weeks later the bluebells. The countryside was a real picture. Spring came and during May Holsworthy staged its annual agricultural show. This is the main event of the year and most of the school children were taking the day off as their parents were involved in some way with the show. Although intending to work as normal Dave decided at the last minute to take a day off, and after obtaining permission from the school for the non attendance of the boys for the day, we all went along to the show. It was a great day out and made a welcome break for Dave.

While we were appreciating all the beautiful things nature has to offer, later in the month we received some sad news from London. A neighbour and good friend of ours had died and although she was elderly it was unexpected. We decided to return to London for the funeral and take a few days off to see the family and old friends. It was nice to have a drink with them all and remember old times but I found I was constantly thinking about the green fields and wondering what flowers had bloomed while we were away. I longed for the peacefulness again, and to think two years ago I didn't even know it existed! In some ways, back in our old circle of friends it seemed we had never been away but I knew in my heart there was only one place I ever wanted to be. When we returned to Bramble Cottage I couldn't wait to see the animals and the garden, nothing seemed to have changed, and then from under the barn door Top Cat came running to greet us. We looked in the barn and amongst the straw were four newborn kittens.

Although late in the day, the last of the sun was still picking out the hills of Dartmoor in the distance, and as I stood there listening to the bird's evening song, I reflected on how just a few hours previously we had been in the heart of London. This was now my home, our home, we had truly come 'OUT OF THE SMOKE'.